Calling Whitetails: Methods, Myths and Magic

GARY SEFTON

Gary Sefton
188 Blue Smith Rd
Cornersville, TN 37047
gsefton37047@yahoo.com

TABLE OF CONTENTS

FOREWORD

"What's that?" the old man said as he pointed to the deer call hanging around my neck. "It's a deer call" I said. "You mean them deer talk?" he asked. I blew a few notes on the call and said "They don't carry on conversations but they do have a limited vocabulary of distinctive sounds that have specific meanings. They use those sounds to communicate with each other so it's kind of like talking". He scratched his head, looked me in the eye and said "I've been deer hunting for 30 years. I ain't never heard a deer say nothing!"

This conversation took place more than 20 years ago in Madison Wisconsin at one of the early "Deer Classics" where I was scheduled to give seminars on deer calling. This "don't make a sound in the deer woods" mindset was fairly typical back then, especially among old time deer hunters but the age of information was gaining ground and deer hunters were beginning to take full advantage of any and every new deer related concept. Deer hunting was fast becoming big business and the market for deer hunting accessories was growing in leaps and bounds, especially those that promised "Big Bucks" with little or no effort.

"Blow the call and get your gun up!" was the sales pitch many call manufacturers used to promote their products and deer hunters, looking for a "magic bullet", couldn't resist. Amazingly enough, without knowing what to say or what they were saying, hunters were having enough success with the calls to keep the momentum going. Deer calls became more popular and the competition among call manufacturers was fierce. The market was driven by "what's new this year" even though deer were still making the same sounds they'd been making for hundreds of thousands of years. Call manufacturers had to keep up with the market demands so, as years went by, new and unique apparatuses and vocalizations were showing up every season with testimonials, magazine articles and the magic of video to validate their claims. Here again, hunters were successful enough, even with bizarre calls with claims like "The Viagra of Deer Calls", to continue the marketing mania, but deer calling tactics are finally coming full circle. A bunch of "revolutionary" new calling concepts have fallen by the way and deer are still communicating in their normal voices. What was effective twenty years ago works just as well today.

I've been in on and part of the deer calling revolution since its infancy, working for game call companies since 1986 doing field testing and research on every aspect of deer calling, including interpreting and dissecting unusual and possibly significant vocalizations. My resume' includes winning the '93, '94 World Deer Calling Championships in Austin, Texas and putting on well over a thousand deer calling seminars from Florida to Oregon and most points in between. There's not much you can do or say to a deer that I haven't tried for experiments' sake and/or in hunting situations and there aren't many reactions to calls I haven't seen. I have called up hundreds of deer using basic techniques and I've probably run as many deer off as I've called up using "latest technology" techniques. The "what's new" frenzy has finally calmed down and we are finally getting back to basics.

The "basics" are what this book is all about. In the following chapters we will concentrate on tactics based on biological facts and scientific observations. Techniques that will work with the most consistency, even though they may not have as much sex appeal as the "Nymphomaniacal Doe Bleat" or the "King Kong Buck Grunt". There are no magic bullets or deer calls made by elves and nothing works every time. Consistency is the best we can hope for and yes, "them deer talk!" Deer calls don't make good deer hunters but they can make good deer hunters better. With proper application, they can be valuable tools and they are here to stay, as well they should be. An accurate deer vocalization done at the right time, in the right place can be the deciding factor in a successful deer hunt.

I. Introduction to Calling; the Magic!

In the Beginning

The reaction was immediate! The crash and dash of a large animal rattled through the woods in response to the sound I'd just made on a duck call look-a-like that was supposed to call deer. The reaction to the call was so sudden and so dramatic I couldn't tell if it was coming to me or running away. I took the revolutionary new "deer call" to a likely spot and followed the instructions to the letter. I made the "burp/grunt" sound with no small amount of trepidation and suddenly he was up and running and blowing and snorting every step of the way. But he wasn't leaving. He was closing ground. He had a head full of horns and a full head of steam and he was coming right at me! I was so flabbergasted by this amazing turn of events; I was totally incapacitated. A dream buck was standing broadside, not 15 yards away, looking right at me and I didn't even raise my bow. I just stood there looking into those blazing eyes that were plainly searching for the intruder who had the nerve to set foot in his domain. Our eyes locked for a split second, and then he wheeled and dashed out of my life forever. He was long gone but 25 years later his memory is still as fresh in my mind as if it happened yesterday. I can't begin to count the number of deer I've called since that day but you never forget your first one. The "Magic" one.

The first one is the Magic One!

After a lifetime of the "silence is golden in the deer woods!" mantra being drilled into my head, I made a guttural "burp" on a reed call and nearly got run over by a sure enough "shooter" buck. This "Grunt Call" as it was appropriately named, was not only a game changer, it was a real "life changer" for me. I was hooked. Any time you can communicate with another species, using their language to manipulate them to your advantage, you have done something real special. I was used to doing it with turkeys and ducks but it never dawned on me to try to call a deer. What a thrill. I knew right then and there I would to try to make that happen again, as often as possible.

A Realistic Approach to Using Deer Calls

We humans attempt to anthropomorphize (give human characteristics to non-human entities) and romanticize the critters we pursue in order to better understand them but.... Deer don't have the same emotional and mental capacities we humans have so we can't accurately judge their perception. We can only go by past experience and the consistency of responses to incidental occurrences. When you are thinking about your deer calling strategies and deciding which call to use, always consider a vocalization's biological purpose. What purpose does it serve? What does the sound mean? What response am I expecting? Is this the right time of the year?

Deer don't make many sounds. They don't carry on conversations or anticipate responses and they don't make any sound for no reason. If they make a sound, it has an intended message and a specific biological purpose. Since deer are social animals, they must be able to communicate with others of their kind in order to maintain cohesion and contact within their social groups. They are surreptitious by nature, avoiding undue attention when possible, so it is no big surprise to say they are not very articulate. Their language is limited to variations of three basic voices; the grunt, the snort and the bleat. They use these three voices in varying degrees of volume and intensity, in distinctive sequences, to convey their most basic desires and emotions to others of their kind. "I'm here, Come here, back off, I'm mad, I'm hungry (fawn mew), I'm lost, Danger, I'm scared" are most of what they have to talk about among themselves, anything else would be redundant and have no real biological purpose. When you hear about "Roars and Growls and Bellows" ask yourself "What unique biological purpose do these those sounds serve. Could deer say the same thing with one of their normal voices?" If a deer makes a sound that doesn't communicate a biological need or purpose or emotion it is most likely an anomaly or a variation of a normal voice caused by stress or physical strain. That is not to say you can't call deer using the "latest, greatest" deer vocalizations. If they are legitimate deer sounds, a rutty buck looking for competition or female companionship might respond to anything that even vaguely resembles a deer sound. We're talking about consistency here. When you make a sound on a deer call you want to be reasonably sure you are "speaking" the normal language with a realistic tone and a specific biological purpose. Time of the year will dictate the sound you make and the response you can anticipate. If you make the right call at the right time you sure won't do any harm and you might very well make some great memories.

Know What You are Saying

Deer respond to calls for reasons dictated by the time of year so it is important to match your calls to the rut phase. In the early pre-rut, bucks are hanging out in bachelor groups and does travel, feed and bed in loosely knit matriarchal groups. At this time their primary interest is in others of their same sex. The sex-specific social grunts and bleats can trigger "social curiosity" responses from members of the groups so; if you want to call bucks you make buck sounds, if you want to call does, make doe sounds. As the fall progresses and testosterone levels rise, bucks get full of themselves and more aggressive toward their running buddies. Social grunt and bleat calls are still effective but responses may be more animated and aggressive. This is also my favorite time to mix in a little light horn rattling with my calls. Bucks start sparring with each other as soon as they shed their velvet. They are always curious about strange bucks in their immediate area. When they hear rattling sounds it means at least two strangers have arrived. I will cover this more thoroughly in my horn rattling chapter but I will say, on several occasions, I have had several bucks show up at one time in response to my rattling in early October.

By mid-November in most parts of the country, the does' estrous cycles are beginning and the bucks are running wild. If they aren't chasing a doe, they are looking for a doe to chase. Prior to the rut, if you wanted to call a buck, you had to sound like a buck. When bucks are looking for does, they will respond readily to doe sounds.

She has him right where he wants her!

That is not to say a buck won't investigate another buck in what is deemed to be his territory, and I use that word loosely. I don't believe a buck marks off an imaginary boundary to establish his territory, I think it more likely his territory is the area immediately surrounding him at the time, wherever he is. Territorial infringement has been the accepted term to describe the aggressive response from one buck to another but a bucks' search for estrous does can be far reaching. No buck could control a territory that size. When a buck responds aggressively to another buck he is defending his dominance or his right to breed a doe and his territory is wherever he is at the time. Depending on the buck to doe ratio where you are hunting, passive and aggressive buck sounds can generate some real exciting responses but the rut is, after all, about breeding does. If you are setting a trap, it makes sense to sound like the bait.

Know What Your Deer Call Should Sound Like

I've gained as much insight from my audiences at the more than a thousand seminars I've given through the years as I have from the deer. There are always stories and questions about sight and sounds audience members see and hear in the deer woods but the most telling information I get from interacting with the folks at the shows is their misconception of what a deer actually sounds like. They have their own perception of what a doe bleat or a buck grunt sounds like, usually gleaned from a TV show where the host was blowing on a call, but very few take the time to research actual deer vocalizations. When I show videos of live deer sounds, the audience is usually amazed by what they hear. Actual buck grunts are never as deep or as loud as perceived and the doe bleats are louder and more pronounced. Most hunters have heard deer grunt in the wild but they don't seem to relate what they hear to what they are sounding like with their calls. They watch the hunting shows on the Outdoor networks and take what they see and hear to heart without question. If they would do a little internet research, they could be listening to the real thing. Even the most internet-challenged individuals can find their way to sites like YouTube, where literally hundreds of short video clips of deer making significant vocalizations can be found. When you watch these clips, be sure you can see the deer making the sounds. Many of the films employ artificial calling that is dubbed in for the sake of convenience or to fit an agenda; you already know what a deer call sounds like, you want to hear the real thing. And don't stop browsing after you hear your first authentic buck grunt. Get on as many sites as you have the time and patience to absorb so you get a good feel for what you should be sounding like when you blow your deer call. Bet you a double cheeseburger you will want to tone down your grunt call.

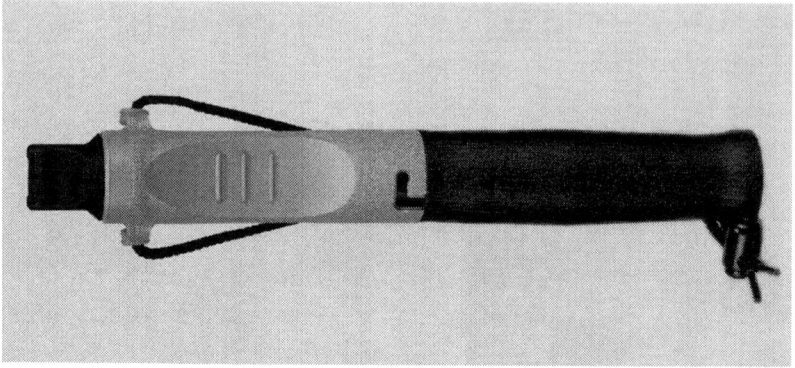

HS Slam Talker Grunt Call

Advantages of Using Deer Calls

Aside from the obvious advantage of making the deer hunt for you, deer calling has some other practical applications and bonuses that you probably haven't considered yet. One of the most important advantages, that very few hunters consider, is the fact that when you use deer calling as an integral part of your hunting strategy, you are coming at the deer from a totally unexpected direction. Blindsiding them! They can smell you, they can see you, they can hear you and they know how to avoid confrontations with you in normal circumstances but nowhere in their mind can they comprehend the fact that you are imitating their language. I've seen the pictures and heard the stories over and over again through the years about the big "unkillable" bucks that were duped by calling and ended up hanging on a wall over somebody's mantle. These four and five year old bucks that went through survival school and passed the course with their hides intact are extra hard to tie a tag on. They are so leery of human contact and so well-tuned to their surroundings, a hunter has very little chance of surprising them with normal hunting practices but….They aren't expecting you to call! And….they are conditioned to respond to conversational deer sounds in predictable ways.

Any response to a deer call is a conditioned response. That is to say, every time a deer investigates a doe bleat they find a doe making the sound. It is the same with buck grunts and rattling horns and any other familiar deer sound. The conditioning is reinforced by repetition so by the time a deer is two years old, he or she knows exactly what to expect when they hear a bleat or a grunt or any other deer sound. When a buck is on the move, looking for a doe to chase, an urgent doe bleat is music to his ears. When he hears another buck grunting and trailing a doe, he knows what that is so he investigates to see if he might be able to take over the chase. When he hears two bucks fighting he beats feet over there to see if he can sneak off with what they are fighting over. These examples of responses to normal deer sounds clearly illustrate an exploitable vulnerability. Just a small chink in their otherwise semi-permeable armor but it's there for us to exploit.

Calling can be the solution to seemingly hopeless hunting situations because you can make the deer hunt for you. You can manipulate him to your advantage by moving him from where he wants to be to where you want him to be by making the right call at the right time.

Even though calling gives you a small foot in the door, you should try to make it easy and convenient for a deer to respond. You know bucks don't like to venture out in open fields in the daylight so don't try to call them into those areas where they are uncomfortable. It can happen, but don't expect a deer to jump a high fence or navigate obstacles to check out your calling. Make it easy on them. A buck would much rather walk a well-used deer trail to investigate your calling than he would an exposed or impassable route so keep that in mind when you set up to call.

Impenetrable thickets that should be big buck sanctuaries are no longer safe havens for them. Set up close to the thicket when the wind is right, make the right call and you have a good chance of coaxing him right out of there. There are no sure things but calling can get the job done when nothing else can. The many great bucks hanging in dens and over fireplaces that would still be out there if they hadn't answered a call, are mute testimony to the fact.

He isn't expecting you to imitate his language.

II. Whitetail Deer Practical Vocabulary

I call this section of the book Practical
Vocabulary because it only deals with sounds familiar
to me. I can comfortably discuss and/or recommend
a sound that has been catalogued by biologists as an
integral part of the language; especially if it is a sound
I have heard often and used to call deer successfully
on more than one occasion. I'll discuss the clicks and
sniffs, the roars, bellows and whistles I hear about so
often from my seminar audiences in a separate chapter
because I'm not sure what they mean or what purpose
they serve. Most of the basic sounds in the
vocabulary can be used to attract deer if used in the
correct sequence and done at the right time on an
accurate device. The purpose of this chapter is to
identify the sounds and their perceived purpose. I will
go into the practical application of the vocabulary in
depth in the methods chapter.

Bleats　Bleat sounds, made by whitetail fawns and does and even bucks, are what I consider to be true vocalizations since they are generated by what can be loosely categorized as "vocal chords" in the deer's larynx. The rest of the deer vocabulary comes from the nasal passages (snorts) and glottal manipulation (grunts). With the exception of the fawn mew which is an appeal to momma at mealtime, bleats communicate varying degrees of stress. The fawn bleat that is used in hunting situations is the distress bleat or bawl a fawn makes when it gets in a frantic situation, when a coyote has him by the leg, for example. Does bleat to tell their fawns to "come here" or to summon others in their maternal groups. The bleat they use in these situations is about two beats in duration "Naaaaht!" nearly monotone, and fairly loud.

Does bleat to call their fawns.

Does will also bleat when they get separated from the group as a communication to re-establish contact. This one is longer –give it three beats, with a rise and fall in pitch."Naaaahhhaaat!" The distinguishing feature of the "lost bleats" is the unmistakable sense of urgency they express. They can be repeated several times (I'll make 5 or 6 in a sequence) keeping the sense of purpose in mind. Does may also use bleats when searching for a temporary husband. When I am trying to hook up with a buck I use the same lost bleats with a little more urgency and in about the same sequence as previously mentioned. When a doe gets involved in a traumatic situation like being hung in a fence or a trap, or when in great pain, her bleat becomes more of a high volume blood curdling bawl that has been extremely disconcerting to me every time I've heard it.

Doe and fawn bleats can be used in hunting situations to attract bucks and does. They can be very effective when used at the right time in the proper sequence. These calling tactics will be discussed in depth in the "Methods" chapter.

Grunts   The grunt is probably the whitetails most expressive voice since it is used in varying degrees of volume and intensity to send several different messages. It seems incongruous to me for a creature with such majestic style and grace to communicate with such an unflattering sound but I guess nature knows best. Biologists have theorized the grunt evolving because the lower frequency carried better and was less reflected in the big woods than a higher pitched voice. For whatever reason, the grunt plays a major role in whitetail communications. The best way to describe the sound is to say it has a clicking quality, much like the sound you get when you run your thumb down the teeth of a plastic comb, one tooth at a time. Think of the comb sound and say "Urp". That is the tone and the duration of most conversational grunts. The more aggressive grunts are longer and louder.

The social doe grunt is the first sound a fawn hears at birth just before he or she gets cleaned up and fed. Does will also use these short, soft grunts to maintain contact and cohesion within their social groups so the doe grunt will always be a positive, reassuring sound. Bucks also make social grunts but the grunt sounds most hunters are familiar with are the "tending" or trailing grunts a buck makes when he is on the track of a doe coming into estrous.

This series of short grunts that sound like a hog coming through the woods are made at varying intervals from one every minute to a grunt every time his foot hits the ground "Uuurrp!---Uuurrp!" Proximity to the doe may dictate the regularity but you couldn't prove it by me. I'm not sure if the bucks are trying to call to the doe and make her stop or just letting her know they are behind her in case she decides to stop. Whatever reason prompts the call, it is the most widely recognized grunt sound because of the volume, the repetition and because it occurs during the time of year when most hunters are in the woods.

Aggressive or aggravated grunt are louder and longer and may rise in pitch and intensity before trailing off "uuurrrRRRrrruuh!" These agonistic and confrontational grunts only occur when two deer of equal stature reach an impasse over something like a preferred food source or the right to breed a doe so they are not as likely to be overheard but aggressive sounds can be productive, given the right situation.

Snorts   If you've never heard a deer snort, you have been deer hunting in the wrong place. The alarm snort of the whitetail deer is far and away the most often heard and easiest recognized deer sound. Snorts are made by exhaling pressured bursts of air through the deer's nasal passages to create loud blowing sounds and the sequence, duration and intensity of the snort determine the message. One sharp blast means you've been positively identified as an imminent source of danger and the snorter is showing you what the hog showed the bear. He's clearing out! The terrified alarm snort usually means the deer got a nose full of human scent. Deer don't question their sense of smell.

In certain situations, a deer will snort repeatedly. If the snorting deer stays in one location, these annoying snorts are called inquiring snorts. They are longer in duration than alarm snorts and they have a questioning quality. The deer thinks something is amiss but is not quite sure and it is trying to get whatever is being snorted at to give its location or identity away. This series of snorts is often accompanied by foot stomping and head bobbing for the same purpose. If the deer had any idea you were a human being trying to reduce it to freezer meat it would be long gone, it wouldn't be hanging around snorting and blowing, and making a fuss.

The aggressive challenging snorts sound much like the alarm snort. They too, are short, loud blasts, but they are repeated over and over. If you are the one being challenged for something you've done with calls or rattling horns, the snorts will be rapidly closing ground. He'll be coming to you with blood in his eyes! It won't happen every time you call but if you are a real deer hunter and you make it happen once, it will be the biggest thrill you'll ever get with all your clothes on and you'll try to make it happen again. If a face to face confrontation with a dominant buck doesn't stand the hair up on the back of your neck you might as well hang it up. Aggravated deer may also make wheezy sniff sounds that are often preceded by aggressive grunts to display anger and aggression. This sound has been catalogued as a "grunt, snort, wheeze" by biologists but it is more of a sequence than a vocalization.

III. Deer Calling Basics (Why Deer Respond to Calls)

They respond to calls at birth.

According to a "seen with my own eyes, first hand observation", deer seem to be born with the ability to respond to vocal instructions. I was driving down a gravel road on my way home from town one spring afternoon when I saw a doe on the side of the road up ahead. She was at least a half mile away but she appeared to be licking something so I slowed down to get a better look. A spindly legged, obviously new born fawn was standing halfway in the road receiving post natal attention from its mother. When the doe saw my truck, she headed for the woods. I was astonished when I noticed the fawn had also disappeared. "Where did it go?" I thought. "It couldn't have run off with her, it's too young. The grass wasn't six inches tall, so it couldn't hide, where did it go?" When I got almost to the spot she had abandoned, it became clear. The fawn, still wet, was halfway out in the edge of the road, hugging the ground. Its feet were splayed out in front and back and its ears were laid low against its neck in an obvious "lay low and be still" position. It never twitched or blinked. The fawn was new born but it must have known instinctively how to "hide in plain sight" and it had to have been acting on a vocal command from the doe. I wouldn't believe it if I hadn't seen it with my own eyes.

Since deer respond to sounds made by other deer throughout their lives, they will respond to artificial calling if you know what to say, when to say it

and what it should sound like. The time of year and
rut phase will dictate the response you can anticipate.
The three basic reasons deer respond to calls are;
social curiosity, dominance (territorial?) infringement and
mating anticipation. I'll talk about the calls that fit the
situations as I explain the responses in the following
chapters.

Social Curiosity

You might be used to seeing deer in groups of
one or two in the fall but deer are actually social
animals. Most of the year they hang out in loosely knit
groups, usually of the same sex. The matriarchal doe
groups are typically made up of related does and their
fawns. The numbers vary but I've seen as many as
fourteen in a bunch and there could easily be more.
These groups will stay together until the does begin
their estrus cycles. Once the breeding phase is over,
they will get back together until early summer when
they start having their fawns.

Bucks prefer the company of other bucks most
of the year. Their bachelor groups, usually containing
as many as six bucks or more, of varying ages, will stay
together until their testosterone builds to an
antagonistic level. Up until that time, while deer are in
these social "herds", they are curious about other deer
in their immediate area, especially those of their same
sex. In the very early fall, passive, social sounds can
arouse their interest enough for them to investigate

the source of the calling. Social curiosity is what I call this pre-rut response, it is sex-specific so if you want to call does you make doe sounds, if you want to call bucks you make buck sounds. The calls that best initiate this response are the non-aggressive social sounds deer use day in and day out to maintain contact and cohesion within their groups. Soft and brief doe or buck grunts have been most productive for me and I like to use them around preferred food sources or loafing areas or well-traveled funnels. These soft grunts not only stimulate curiosity, they also serve as an "all clear" signal to let any deer within hearing know it is safe to come into an area. On many occasions I have calmed down nervous deer that were a flag's twitch away from full flight with a soft doe or buck grunt. I also preface any calling or rattling sequence with one or two of the low volume grunts because they seem to put deer at ease. If I can talk to a relaxed deer, I have a chance to call him. If he has one ear to the ground trying to figure out which way to go to save his life, A. T.&T couldn't call him. The call that I think most accurately reproduces the doe grunt is an ingenious friction operated device that was made by Woods Wise.

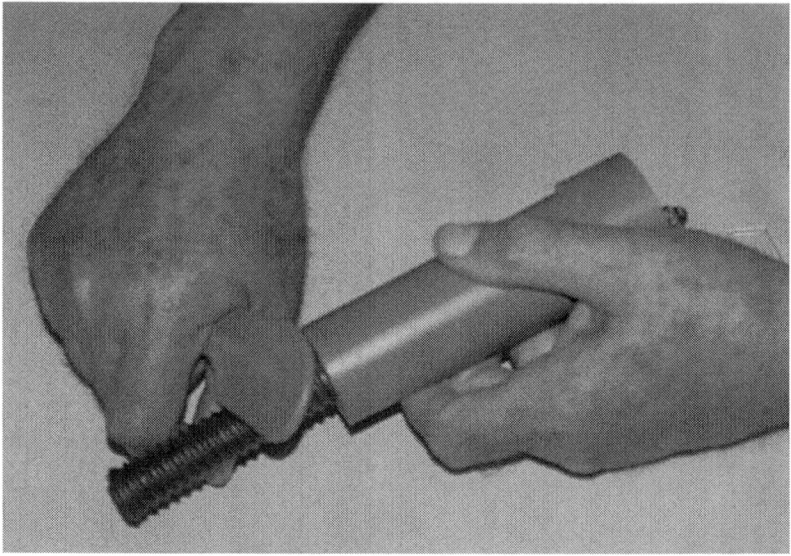

Friction Grunt Call

I'm not sure if it is still in production but I still have mine and I'll use it 'til I lose it since I don't think you can wear one out. It is the most accurate grunt call I've heard, especially at the lower volumes and the higher pitches that characterize doe grunts and young buck social grunts. The tip of the call adjusts in and out for lower or higher pitched tones and the volume is controlled by the amount of pressure you put on the striker/paddle. It is a little unwieldy since it takes two hands to operate but I'm in agreement with my old friend, the late Doug Camp when he said "heck, I'd carry a brick in my pocket if I thought it would do any good.".

I usually give "off mike" demonstrations of the call in my seminars to give the attendees a true perspective on the volume of the sound. I had just finished a demonstration in Ohio when a guy in the front row said "They sure don't talk very loud!" I said "No, they don't, but deer have ears this long (I spread my hands to six inches) and they have one of them on each side of their head. They are listening for that sound. They are tuned to that frequency." Deer can only make three sounds. They change the volume and sequence of the sounds to send different messages. You can say hey, or HEY! for example. Same word but the increased volume gives it a totally different meaning.

The current marketing campaigns for buck ROARS! and GROWLS! and BELLOWS! have fostered some misconceptions about the volume of deer communications. I think those loud calls work on bucks that are so wired up they will respond to anything that sounds like a deer. In normal circumstances, any loud deer sound you hear or make on your call is a frustrated sound, an aggressive sound or an all-out alarm. None of these conveyed emotions are consistently attractive to deer so keep the volume down for the social sounds. "How often do you make that sound?" The guy in the front row asked. "Once or twice every ten or fifteen minutes in a high deer use area." I said. "The soft grunts are social sounds and they don't bear repeating. It would be like you hearing a man saying Hello, Hello, Hello, Hello and on and on. You know what's making the sound and you know what he is saying but it makes you nervous when he says it over and over. Deer are already nervous enough without exposing them to unnatural sequences." The brief "come here" doe bleats can also be used to arouse social curiosity but, here again, keep them soft and they don't bear repeating. If you are hunting over a white oak tree that is dropping acorns you will probably have both sexes show up under the tree at different times to feed whether you call or not. It is still a good idea to make some soft calls. Deer don't make social sounds if they are stressed or nervous about anything so the reassuring sounds not only let other deer know it is safe to come into an area, it relaxes the deer that are responding so they show up in their normal feeding mode.

Deer are social animals most of the time.

Just for your information, in my many years of hunting over acorn trees, I have noticed the does usually come in first to feed under the oaks. The bucks come later. I'm not sure if it is a "ladies first" courtesy or the fact that the bucks have figured out the squirrels knock the nuts out of the trees later in the morning. In any case, if you are hunting bucks, wait until the does wander off, then do some soft buck grunts. Keep in mind you are not trying to summon another deer. You are more or less broadcasting your presence and situation to any deer that might be checking out the area. "I'm over here and everything is alright" is the message you're sending.

As the season progresses, the response can be more aggressive and more about dominance infringement than social curiosity, even though you are sending the same message. A relaxed buck is still an intruder. Even if the response is more aggressive, you convinced a deer to investigate your calling and that is about all you can ask for. Social curiosity is an inherent aspect of the whitetail persona that is present to some degree year round. It is there for you to exploit if you can be in the right place and make the right call.

Bachelor group of bucks.

They like each other!

Maternal Instinct Response (Involuntary?)

"Maaaaaaaaaaaaa!" "Maaaaaaaaaaaa!" the terrified shrieks rang out in desperation as they shattered the tranquility of a late summer afternoon. The video camera focused on an unfortunate fawn that had been in the wrong place when a farmer was cutting hay. "Maaaaaaaaaaaaa!" The fawn screamed again." The camera panned over to a young boy with a pained expression on his face. "Daddy that hurts my ears!" The boy said as he covered both ears with his hands. "And look, there's his momma! There are 2 mommas!" he pointed as the camera panned to the edge of the field where 2 does nervously stomped and bobbed their heads. They were obviously trying to decide whether or not to proceed to the location of the distress calls in spite of the crowd of people and equipment at the source of the sound. This vivid encounter came to me in an unsolicited video tape from a deer hunter in West Virginia. It was too graphic to include on a commercial video but it clearly illustrates the volume of the fawn distress bleat and its' effect on mature does.

By imitating the same agonized bleats, you can attract does in dramatic fashion, right up to the time when their estrus cycle begins. The does distance themselves from their fawns once the bucks start chasing them since rutting bucks can pose a real threat to the youngsters. I have called many does with fawn bleats on purpose and nearly as many unintentionally with predator calls. I'm not sure what a doe plans to do when she gets to the distressed fawn but she gets there in a hurry and she looks like she is ready to do battle. I don't think the doe can distinguish the sound of her own fawns distress cries from other fawn cries or if it even makes any difference, as witnessed in the aforementioned tape. Two does responded to the fawn cries that afternoon and at least one of them was unrelated. Since it is an apparently random response to an urgent distress call, I have to believe it is an involuntary knee-jerk response to a frantic situation. If you want to see a dramatic call-up, take a fawn bleat with you on a late September hunt and blow the heck out of it. You can't do it too loud or too long. It is a can 'til can't call since a fawn will start squalling when it gets in trouble and it won't stop until it gets out of trouble or can't squall any more. After you make the calls, be ready to shoot. The doe will come in fast and she will usually leave just as fast.

Her maternal instinct is strong!

Mating Anticipation

This is the one that has the potential to get us all in trouble. The inherent aptitude to reproduce is one of the most powerful urges in the animal kingdom, often clouding an individual's instinct for survival. As the daylight hours get shorter, the buck's testosterone levels increase and the doe estrus cycles begin and the rut is on. A four or five year old buck that is normally the square root of paranoid will throw caution to the winds when a hot doe shows up. He will be relentless in his pursuit of the fairer sex while tolerating no interference from his peers. This propensity to reproduce is the mature buck's major weakness and it can be exploited with calls. This is where an accurate doe bleat call can save the day.

The bleats does use to call to their fawns and to maintain contact within their social groups can also be used to make contact with bucks. This possibility first came to my attention over forty years ago in Florida when Jim Pennington, long gone hunting buddy and early mentor told me about the run-in his wife Marge had with a rutty buck up in Ocala's Big Scrub. He said "Marge always had an orphan fawn or two that she would shut up and bottle feed until they got old enough to take care of themselves. She kept them in the barn about 200 yards from the house and fed them twice a day. She learned to imitate the sounds does used to call to their fawns so she could talk to her young'uns a little and let them know when she was coming. One bright moonlit night, as she walked down the old sand road to the barn, she let out a couple bleats to let the fawns know she was on her way. All of a sudden, the biggest buck she'd ever laid eyes on jumped into the sand road and squared off, face to face, right in front of her. Scared the curlers right out of her hair! I mean she tore up the road gettin' back to the house." He said. "She kept her mouth shut when she was feeding at night after that." I got a good laugh out of the story and I didn't attach much significance to it until I started using deer calls.

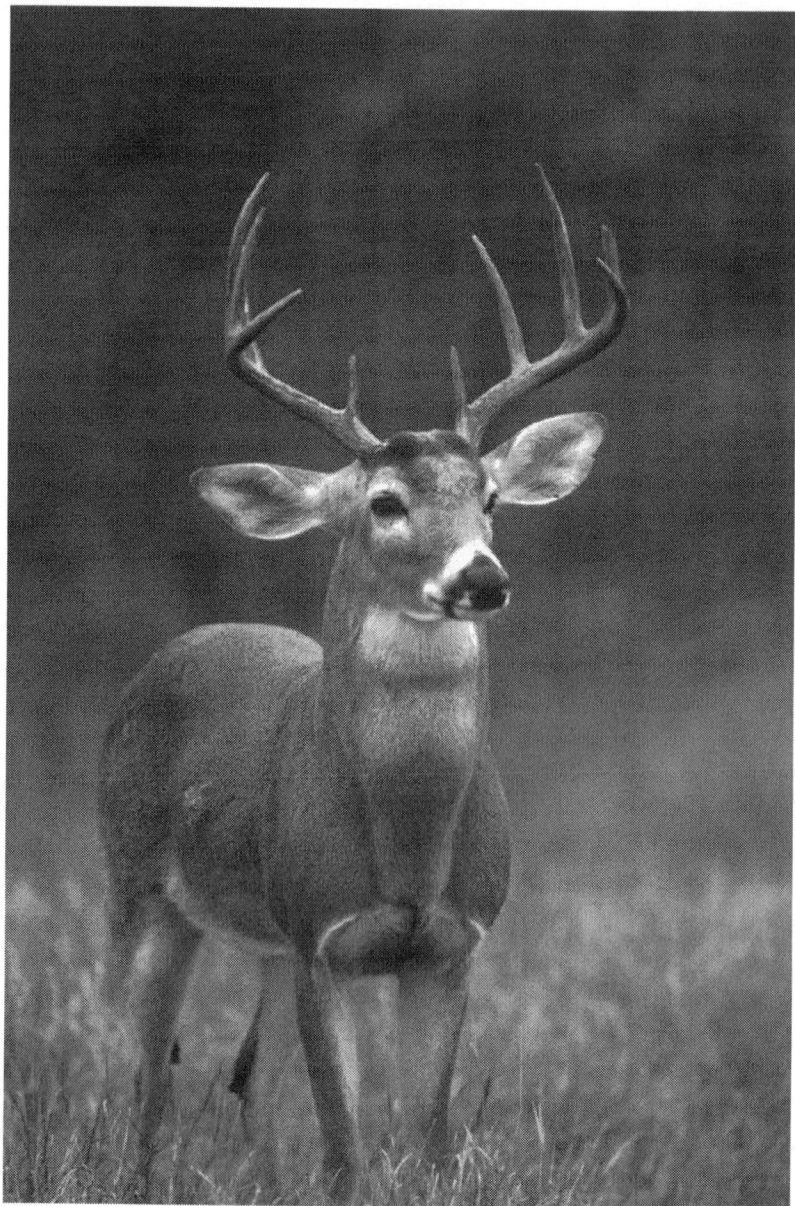

Scared the curlers right out of her hair!

An actual estrus doe bleat has not been documented to my knowledge but it doesn't matter. When a buck is looking for a doe, he will come to any doe sound. I don't think he cares what she is saying. Doe grunts can also be effective for the same reason and, strange as it may sound, many of the responses to horn rattling are the result of mating anticipation.

When a buck comes to investigate the sounds made by two bucks fighting, I don't think he comes to fight the winner and get his head all skinned up. I think it more likely he knows they are fighting over something and he comes to see if he can slip off with the prize while they are otherwise occupied. He will respond for the same reason to the tending or trailing grunt sounds a buck makes while he is trailing an estrus doe. When a buck hears a series of grunts moving through the woods he knows what it means and, depending on his stature in the pecking order, he may want to join in the chase and compete for the prize. Speaking of "tending grunts", I believe the term is a misnomer. To my thinking, tending is the actual breeding process. The term is catchier and has more sex appeal than trailing but I have seen several bucks breed does. The act is, in a word, brief. There is no time for conversation or pillow talk so I think "trailing grunt" better describes the sound a buck makes while he is trailing a doe.

He's trailing and he's grunting!

The rut is all about sex and violence and it gets hot and heavy during the "peak" phase. Propagating the species is job one and foremost on the agenda of both sexes. Bucks are up to their eyes in testosterone and driven hard, night and day, to make contact with as many receptive does as possible. They are so single-minded and intense in their pursuit they forego much of their normal caution which makes them more likely to make mistakes in judgment. This small blip in their normally evasive behavior is there for you to exploit and the peak of the rut is your best window of opportunity. This is the time of year when bucks are eager to respond to anything that comes close to sounding like a deer but you will be more consistent if you stick to the basics. Doe bleats, doe grunts, buck grunts and horn rattling work just as well now as they did twenty years ago and they can all be effective during the rut so try to be in the woods at this magic time of the year.

The Mechanics of Calling Deer

The trick to calling anything is knowing what to say, when to say it and what it should sound like. The preceding chapters contain most of that information but you will need more than precise written descriptions of the actual and the artificial sounds. Once again, I direct you to google deer vocalizations and listen to the live deer recordings. Once you know what a vocalization should sound like, you will need an accurate device to reproduce the sounds. I can make suggestions now that I don't work for call companies but different ears hear different sounds. My best advice is to listen to different grunt and bleat calls and go with the ones that sound best to your ear in comparison to what you've heard on "live" shows and tapes.

Social Curiosity Situations (Early Season Calling)

Late September and early October are my favorite times to bow hunt whitetails. I look forward to my pre-season scouting trips in search of preferred food sources and I enjoy the satisfaction and the beginning tingles of apprehension I have when I find what I am looking for. I use binoculars to scout for acorns (they can hide from the naked eye) and mark the heavy nut bearers on a map before the season. I always revisit the marked sites before I hang stands to make sure the trees are dropping acorns and the deer have found them. Knowing the deer are going to feed heavily at some time of the day gives me the confidence I need to hang in and stay put. Not knowing what is going to show up under the trees keeps me awake and alert enough to stay on the stand until I can't see my feet.

This is also a great time to use deer calls to exploit a deer's inherent sense of curiosity about other deer. As discussed in previous chapters, deer are social animals. They are comfortable and secure in their matriarchal and bachelor groups and they are curious about others of their kind, especially those of their same sex. This knowledge gives us a small foot in the door and an opportunity to use the passive social sounds to encourage deer to investigate our calling.

Doe Contact Grunts

As earlier mentioned, a soft doe contact grunt is a reassuring sound to either sex since the first time they hear it they get cleaned up and fed. It is also a relaxing sound that makes an encouraging statement to all who hear it. The soft doe grunt establishes the fact that there is at least one unstressed deer in the immediate area. And don't forget, these contact grunts are not loud or repeated often. If deer made social grunts often, with any volume, you would be hearing them all over the woods. I talked about doe grunts in an earlier chapter but this aspect of calling is so important, it bears repeating. I use the friction grunt to make very soft calls, once or twice every ten or fifteen minutes. The sound is also short in duration. Think "urp!" And you have the length of the grunt down. If you make two grunts, the second one is for you. The deer heard you the first time. When you wait ten or fifteen minutes between calls, you are hopefully calling to new arrivals in the area. Remember, you are not necessarily trying to summon a deer to your call; you are just trying to pique their curiosity and let them know the area is safe. You are talking to yourself more than to others. You're just saying I'm over here and everything is alright.

Buck Contact Grunts

Soft buck contact grunts can also pique the curiosity of bachelor group bucks while they are still hanging out with their buddies. Just remember the length and duration of the doe grunt for your pattern; short and sweet. You are just getting their attention and I don't think they are that particular about the tone as long as you keep the sequence natural. You can tone down adjustable-reed grunt calls to simulate serviceable doe and young buck grunts as long as they maintain that "clicky" quality that is characteristic of all deer grunts.

E-Z Grunter Extreme

I can suggest you try the Knight & Hale E-Z Grunter Extreme if you are confused by the choices. It makes excellent soft buck grunts with a minimum amount of air pressure and it also makes decent doe bleats when you inhale on it. Variable pitch calls are also available that allow the caller to change the tone of the call by twisting the barrel or pushing a button in the right place or moving an "o" ring. If you have a variable call, find what you think is the right sound and lock it in so it will be the same every time. A man with one watch knows what time it is, if he has two watches, he isn't sure. You have to be the judge of what sounds best to you but this is not the time or place for the "King Kong" buck grunts "as seen on TV". There will be a time when loud aggressive grunts can get results but for now you're just saying everything is alright. No need to sound like somebody trying to "crank a chain saw" as one of my seminar attendees described the sound his grunt call made. It is human nature to think more and bigger is better but not so with passive deer calling. When you turn one of those monster buck grunts loose in the woods you are saying "I'm over here and I weigh 900 Pounds!" No buck in his right mind is going to respond to a loud, deep grunt like that in a relaxed fashion. Even if he thinks he's tough enough to investigate, he'll want to know more about this loudmouth. He will invariably go downwind to scent check the intruder. Game over! for the caller. I believe there are more good bucks run off with "Thunder Buck" grunt calls the caller wasn't even aware of, than are successfully called up. Remember, "social curiosity" is the response we're after in the early season. Deer are interested and curious about others of their same sex and a Boone & Crockett buck is just as curious and concerned about a fork horn as he would be about another B&C in his immediate area.

So, in an ideal early season situation, we set up in a high deer use area close to a preferred food source or frequently traveled funnel and call sparingly. Soft and brief is the formula, "Urp!…Urp!". Wait ten to fifteen minutes and call again, same formula. It's alright to vary the time between calls. There is no real sequence as long as you don't call too often. That would turn your calling into an unnatural sequence. As previously mentioned, unnatural sequences make everything nervous!

IV. Calling During the Rut (Mating Anticipation)

Hormones rule during the rut. When bucks' senses are steamed up with testosterone and his nose is full of estrous scent he will be less wary than at any other time. When you start seeing bucks lying dead beside the highway, you can bet the rut is "on". This is the only time a buck will throw caution to the wind and proceed with reckless abandon, putting himself in harms' way by doing foolish things like running out in traffic on a busy highway in his single-minded pursuit of female companionship. A buck's apparent increased vulnerability during this time will also make him more susceptible to calling if you can catch him between affairs.

Hooking up with an unengaged buck during the peak of the rut can be problematical in many states because of the highly skewed doe to buck ratios. For many years, most states enacted "buck only" regulations to build the herd by protecting the does. Since bucks and does are born in a 1 to 1 ratio and no does were harvested during this prolonged period, a huge imbalance was created in those states. When wildlife agencies realized what was happening, they initiated doe harvest quotas but they were mostly too little and too late and some hunters are still hesitant about shooting does so the numbers remain lopsided. You can make does legal game and issue as many doe tags as you want but you can't make hunters shoot them.

Even in those states with an overabundance of does, the rut is still a great time to trick a buck with a call, especially in the early phase. Remember, he has been spending all of his time with a bachelor group of hairy-legged males for the past eight or nine months. He has had little or no contact with the opposite sex and the days are getting shorter and the testosterone levels are surging and all of a sudden, he's rarin' to go, even if the majority of the does aren't! This creates a competitive atmosphere among the whitetail ranks and an ideal situation for a deer caller. This is what I call the chasing stage, when the basket racks and fork horns are harassing every doe they can scare up while the older, more experienced bucks bide their time. The trick here is to figure out where a buck is biding his time so you can make him an offer he can't refuse.

Bedding areas and thickets at the ends of scrape lines are good places to consider when you are scouting for call set-ups and preferred food sources are always good choices. When you are hunting experienced bucks you should take extra precautions. Don't set up too close to the target area and be sure you can get in and out of your stand undetected. During this brief period you can call bucks with doe or buck sounds and you can expect enthusiastic responses to either one.

Trailing Grunts

I like to focus my attention in the late October, early November pre-rut season on hunting bucks so I start my calling sequences with buck grunts. I try to provoke a mating anticipation and/or a social curiosity response with what I call "trailing grunts"; short monotone grunts that sound kind of like a hog coming through the woods "uuhhrrp!---uuhhrrp!". To add some realism that is mostly for my own self-satisfaction, I vary the volume and direction to give the impression of a buck on the move. I'll do two minute sets of these grunts and repeat them every five or ten minutes hoping a dominant buck comes within hearing. This calling sequence should be interpreted by any buck in the area to mean a strange buck is close by and he is following a soon to be receptive doe. This is a situation that should get his immediate attention! If he responds, he could come in quick and animated, ready to put the stranger in his place or he could circle downwind to scent-check the situation. That's not to say a buck won't investigate doe bleats at this time but I like to keep them as my hole cards in case I don't get any action from the buck grunts.

Staying close!

When the scrapes you've been watching fill up with leaves and go untended, the rut should be in full swing. The mature bucks that have been checking and refreshing the scrapes on a regular basis are now too busy chasing does to mess with pawing the ground but they are most likely still in the area. They might seem reclusive because they are usually hanging close to a receptive doe.

A buck will stay with her as long as she stays receptive (usually 24 hours) or she slips away. During this period I have had more success with doe bleats. I think an urgent doe bleat is a more compelling invitation than an aggressive or challenging buck grunt, especially when a buck is casting around looking for a doe that was "here just a minute ago".

She's around here somewhere!

Doe Bleats

When she talks, they listen!

As earlier stated, does use bleat sounds to call to their fawns and to communicate with others in their same sex, matriarchal groups. Bleats usually denote some kind of stress and their sequence, volume and duration signal the degree of urgency. Come here right now, I'm lost, or I'm in a world of hurt are common usages. It has been said a doe will bleat to try to make contact with a buck when she is at the peak of her estrous cycle. It makes perfect sense to me, especially since I have called several dandy bucks in during the rut using doe bleats.

In high doe to buck ratio areas, it is not at all uncommon for a doe to go unbred for two and three estrus cycles. This is not from a lack of effort on her part. She knows it is in her best interest to conceive as early in the year as possible so her fawns can have more time to grow, giving them their best chance to survive a hard winter. When her cycle begins, she will broadcast her urgency through her urine deposits, her glandular secretions and apparently through her vocal signals. Again, I can't say there is a bleat that is specifically associated with breeding because I haven't seen documentation of such a sound and bleats are used by does year round when there is no breeding activity going on. My personal success along with numerous successful hunt stories passed on by other hunters calling bucks with doe bleats make a good case for the likelihood of does using bleats to make contact with bucks. It could be that a buck knows he has to be where the does are in order to pass on his genetic material so…. when he hears a doe bleat, no matter what she is saying, he goes to her. When I am trying to attract a buck with bleats I do much more animated versions of the doe lost contact bleats. This louder and longer series of bleats rise and fall in tone and intensity and send a more urgent message than the normal lost contact bleats. The short "come here" bleat is more of a nahh! The lost bleat is longer and more animated naaahaaahh!

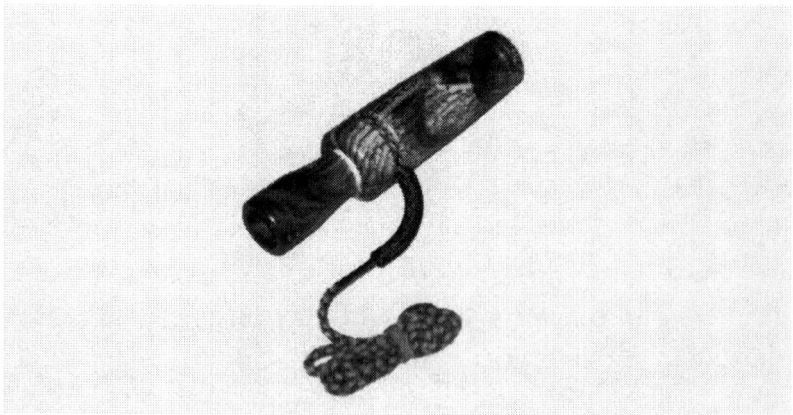

Doe Bleat Call

Here again you can source Google for some examples of live doe bleats, then try the calls until you find one you like. If you want something that is automatic, you might try the tip or bleat cans.

Can Call

These cans were originally used for the internal sound mechanisms in toys so dolls could say mama when you rocked them. When somebody rocked a doll and thought it sounded like a deer bleat, a new calling device was created. Because of their simplicity and their original toy application, it took deer hunters awhile to accept them as plausible and realistic deer calls but......Amazing success stories and good marketing, along with the fact that a bleat can was inexpensive and the perfect "no-brainer" deer call, soon created a large demand. Bleat cans are still quite popular and hunters are still enjoying success with them, possibly due to sheer numbers in the field. I don't believe the canned bleats will alarm deer and success stories abound so it won't hurt to give them a try. Do three or four evenly spaced can bleats, wait awhile, then repeat the sequence. Even though the tone and volume are set on a bleat can, if you will "think deer" while you are making the calls, I believe it will make your calling more realistic.

The advantage of using a reed call over the one dimensional bleat can is the ability to change the dynamics and the volume of the call and put more emotion into your calling. Since there is always some urgency involved with bleats, the natural sequence is to repeat the sound several times at a pretty good volume, here again, visualizing what you would sound like if you were trying to attract or communicate a need to another deer. Think urgent doe when you call and stay ready. If nothing shows up, wait ten minutes and try again.

Fawn Distress Bleats

Using fawn distress bleats to appeal to the

maternal instinct of mature does was discussed briefly in the vocabulary section but the sequence and volume and duration along with what the call should sound like bears repeating. The duration of a distress call is unlimited. A fawn starts squalling when it gets in trouble and doesn't quit until it can't squall anymore or it gets out of trouble. Fawn bleat calls are available from most call manufacturers and they sound pretty much alike so take your pick, as long as the call has enough volume. It should be loud enough to "hurt your ears", to paraphrase the youngster quoted in the vocabulary section. Just voice a long "maaaaaaa!" as you blow the call and repeat it every other breath with all the urgency you can muster. Wail and scream on the call like there is no tomorrow, 15 or 20 times. If nothing shows up, wait five minutes and repeat the sequence. When a doe responds, she will usually come on the run but she will also leave on the run so be ready with your bow or gun. A doe charging your position with her hair standing on end and her eyes on fire is something to remember.

The "maternal instinct" response is pretty consistent in late summer and early fall but it is also perplexing to me. I have seen does leave their fawns and come to distress calls on several occasions and I have seen two and three does come to the call from different directions, all at the same time. This response is apparently not confined to related offspring and I'm not sure what a doe would do if she responded to a distress call and found a big old bear holding the fawn, even if it was her own flesh and blood. Also, hard charging responses to fawn distress bleats don't seem to fit the does' fight or flee biological profile. To add to my confusion, I have called nearly as many does in with dying rabbit cries while predator hunting as I have with fawn bleat calls.

But I have never called a buck with fawn bleats. That is not to say it can't happen. I have heard several stories from what I consider to be reliable sources, about dramatic buck responses to fawn bleats that I won't refute. I'm just saying...I have spent more time blowing the bleats than most and it hasn't happened to me. Since bucks don't raise fawns, they don't seem to be concerned with their well-being. A testosterone soaked buck might follow a doe that is responding to a distress call or, he might be confusing the distress calls with estrus doe bleats. Whatever the reason, it is an uncommon response for a buck. You don't want to base your calling strategies on uncommon responses.

Calling with Snorts??

Of the three kinds of snorts we talked about in the vocabulary chapter, the alarm snort was the only one that said "I'm Outta Here Right Now!" The challenging snort dares you to come and fight while the inquiring snort indicates a state of high alert and cautious curiosity.

When you hear long, drawn out snorts with a questioning quality, repeated over and over, it means a nosey old doe(if she hangs around long, you can bet it is a doe) thinks she smells a rat but she isn't sure what or where. You're not going to do much good hunting with an old doe telling the whole world there is some kind of a booger in your area so you need to do something to turn off the sound. Your best bet is to try to call her up or at least try to calm her down with doe grunts or bleats that let her know you are just another deer.

I was once advised to snort back at the snorting doe to let her know I was another deer. When I tried snorting back, the result was a long, loud snorting contest. I was answering a stress sound with another stress sound so when I would snort, she would snort back at me; every time. That went on long enough to terrorize the whole countryside. If you want a nosey doe to think you're a deer, try doe grunts or a couple "come here" bleats. She will still know what you are and you will be sending her a reassuring message that should calm her down. Once the old tattletale realizes her "rat" is just another deer, she will usually go on about her business and let the woods get back to normal.

She smells a rat!

Some unusual circumstances have led me to believe slightly altered snorts may communicate even more subtle messages. On several occasions I have watched deer feeding and loafing in front of my stand and heard deer snorting, for whatever reason, not too far away. The deer usually paid no attention to the distant snorts but once in a while, in response to what sounded like the same snorts; they would tear out of there like something was chasing them. On one occasion, I heard a deer snorting just over the ridge, directly downwind from me. I was sure the snorting deer was fussing about the occasional whiff of my scent the wind carried to her but three does and two yearlings that were feeding close to my stand didn't even look up. The next time they heard a deer snort, the sound came from much farther away. This time they hoisted their flags and cleared out. I have also seen deer attracted to snorting deer several times and I have heard many does snort as they were being pursued by passionate bucks.

I was hunting a huge cornfield in Central Illinois one mid November evening when I saw a buck milling around at the far end of the field. He was so far away I had to use my binoculars to make sure he was a "shooter". He was much too far to hear any of my conventional deer calls but daylight was fading fast. I wanted to do something to try to bring him to my end of the field so I got out my snort call and did my best to mimic the snorts I'd heard does make when bucks were after them. The buck threw his head up and came all the way across the field at a fast trot.

On another occasion, I was still hunting through some overgrown crop fields in Tennessee after an unusual Mid-November snow fall when I happened up on a small, willow choked stock pond. Fresh deer tracks were all around the pond and nearly every willow tree in the area was skinned up with fresh rubs. This "hot spot" looked so promising I walked around the pond twice, checking the sign and trying to figure out how to hunt it. I was standing on the pond dam, about eight feet above the rest of the landscape, getting ready to move on when an inspiration struck me. I blew hard into my balled up fist, making the loudest snort I could muster without the aid of a call and a loud, brush thrashing, limb breaking scramble immediately ensued. A heavy horned buck came boiling out the pond heading for the wild blue yonder. I was so startled and so rattled; I shot my rifle dry without cutting a hair as he fled across the wide open, snow covered fields. That's my excuse and I'm sticking to it! Older bucks will sometimes hold tight to avoid human contact.

A loud alarm snort is so unexpected it can surprise a reclusive buck right out of his lay-low strategy. Keep that in mind when you are slipping around in the deer woods.

Caught me off guard; that's my story!

The most aggressive deer vocalization, I believe, is a nasally generated sniff-wheeze. It is a compressed snort sound that is sometimes preceded by a full blown snort. It is then called a snort-sniff-wheeze. The sniff-wheeze sequence can also be started off with an aggravated grunt which is then catalogued as a grunt-sniff –wheeze. When you hear either one, you are listening to a mad deer. This is the last sound a deer will make before he or she (does will sniff wheeze when annoyed) goes into violent physical action. It is more of a final warning than a challenge by bucks and does in confrontational situations such as disputes over a preferred food source or the right to breed a doe. This super aggressive call sequence was touted as an attractive sound by call companies at one time and it can get a dominant buck's curiosity stirred up enough to investigate the caller if he is the stud buck and he is in the right mood but it can also clear an entire area of all deer, with that one exception.

Snort calls can be effective in certain situations but you have to be careful about the message you send. You can be sure the snorts all convey some degree of stress which can result in a negative response or a down-wind investigation. As I said earlier, I don't understand all I know about deer snorts. When I'm not sure about what I'm saying, I don't say much.

Most major call companies manufacture some kind of a snort call, usually bundled with an aggressive grunt call for your "grunt-sniff-wheeze" convenience. Most of these "snort calls" employ "blow in the hole" technology which can do a fair job though you can get nearly the same results blowing through your fist or any small aperture that will compress an exhaled breath. The best snort calls I have found use a reed to contribute to the sound and volume. I'm not sure who makes this type anymore; you'll have to ask before you buy. I don't want to get blamed for teaching folks how to run deer off so I use a snort call for demonstrations in seminars to identify the different meanings but I hold off on any ringing endorsements for their use in hunting situations. Snorts can be effective in highly specialized situations but I think I can say, with some degree of certainty, there are as many deer run off with snort calls as are actually called up.

V. Horn Rattling

I remember me and my high school buddies reaction to a scene from the Robert Mitchum movie "Home from the Hill" way ack when. One of the characters was out in the woods, beating two deer antlers together, expecting a buck to show up. We laughed long and hard and thought that was one of the most ridiculous things we'd ever seen come out of Hollywood. We could accept "Creature from the Black Lagoon" and "Godzilla" but we were deer hunters. We knew you couldn't expect to see a deer if you were making a lot of noise, no matter what you were making it with. If I had only known, back in 1960 when that scene took place, what I know now, I could have been way ahead of the game. I'm sure horn rattling has been used in some form to attract bucks since Moby Dick was a minnow, especially out in Texas where deer seem to be more aggressive, but it

took me more than twenty years to realize the
potential East of the Mississippi.

"Most of my rattling is done twenty feet off of the ground!"

Sparring

They're just playing!

As soon as the bucks shed their velvet, they start sparring with others in their bachelor groups, to establish dominance and sort out a pecking order. They push and shove each other around, back off, then lock up and push again. Nothing violent, they just test each other's mettle and practice up for the real thing. This is a common occurrence in the deer woods as autumn approaches so the sound made by the antlers clashing is normal and non-threatening to other deer. Since deer are interested in others of their kind, when they hear the antlers rubbed together they are curious about the two strangers sparring in their area. Yes, the response to horn rattling in the early fall is…social curiosity. As the days get shorter testosterone levels rise and the sparring gets more heated. When the bucks start hurting each other, they quit hanging out together. When the bachelor groups break up, the rut is on.

Most does are not receptive when the rut begins so competition can be fierce for those that cycle early. Bucks of equal stature can get in serious fights over the right to breed during this time so you can be more aggressive with your rattling sequences if you prefer, but be sure to keep an eye down wind. And you can expect the response to be way more dramatic. This is the one that makes the hair on the back of your neck stand up and your heart beat so hard you can't swallow. When a big horned buck comes charging right at you with smoke coming out of his nose and his eyes on fire, you'll have to make a special effort just to remember to draw your bow!

Conventional wisdom used to say you need big racks to rattle up big bucks. Conventional wisdom finally gave way to common sense. When hunters considered the fact that antler size couldn't be determined by and didn't even matter to an aggressive buck checking out the competition, they realized how awkward a pair of horns could be in a tree stand. To satisfy this need, the market for alternative rattling devices was born. Today, devices on the market designed to replicate the sound of clashing antlers range from synthetic antler replicas to rattling bags, to elaborate machines and remote controlled mechanical devices. And they all work, some better than others. Deer aren't that particular. I talked to one hunter who, unintentionally, rattled up a buck by tapping an arrow on his quiver. Another who got the surprise of his life when a buck came storming in to the sound he made pounding on a tree step.

Rattle Bag

Choose the rattling device that you find to be the most convenient but it should also sound good to you. As I said, I don't think deer are that particular but if you don't think your rattling sounds authentic, you won't have the confidence you need to be consistently successful. I've had about the same amount of success with bags and mechanical devices as I have with real horns. The advantage of the bags and devices over the real thing is in the ease of transporting and manipulating them in close quarters in a blind or on a tree stand. And there is the safety aspect; the devices won't hurt you if you fall on them and they don't look like the first thing that makes a hunter take his safety off (an antler!). If you are going to use antlers I strongly recommend sawing off the antler tips. If you don't, I can just about guarantee, at some point, you will wish you had.

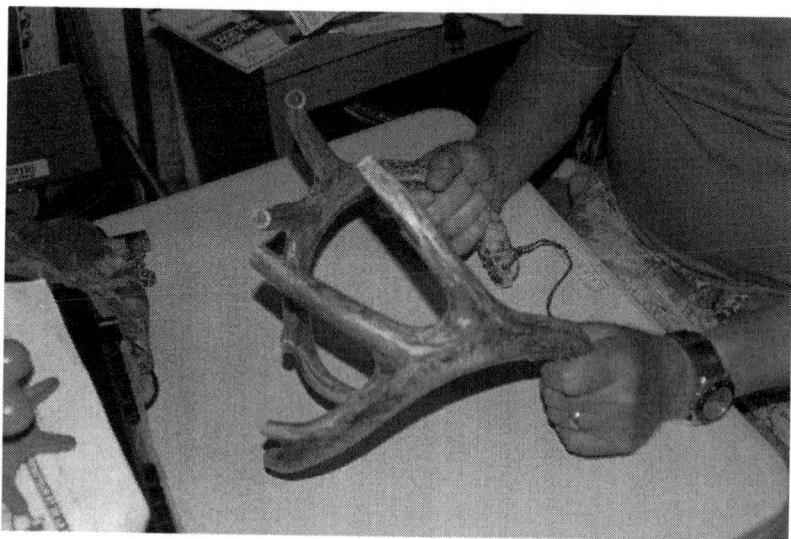

Saw off sharp tips!

The handiest and most realistic rattling device I've found is the Knight & Hale "Pack Rack". It takes up very little space in your pack and the realism and volume are more than adequate.

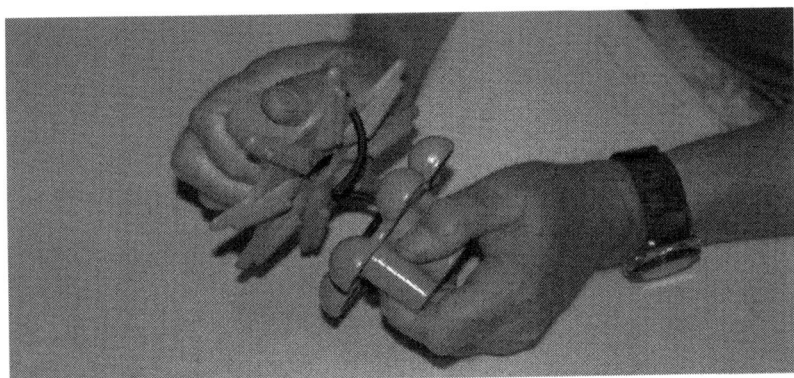

Pack Rack

Another "conventional wisdom myth" involves the physical location of the person doing the rattling and the typical sequence. Most of the hunting "personalities", especially those selling synthetic antler replicas, tell their readers and listeners "The first thing you do, to begin your rattling sequence, is WHACK! the horns together; to get his attention! You whack those horns together like that; the next thing you have to do is call him back from where ever you ran him off to when you whacked the horns together. That whack is nothing but a loud, violent sound that doesn't send any message to a deer other than "flee and try to figure out if a tree fell or two cars ran together out on the highway".

Sparring sequences are non-violent confrontations. Keep that in mind when you are rattling. They push and shove and tickle the tines in sporadic sequences; stop and start. There is no right or best way to perform sparring sequences; there is no set rhythm or technique. You can't go wrong if you just imagine what two bucks would sound like that weren't really trying to hurt each other. Tickling tines and gently grinding horns is the sound you are after on whatever rattling device you are using. This is the familiar sound that triggers the "curiosity" response. No Whacks! Nothing else! You can break limbs and thrash leaves and stomp around until sweat is sloshing in your Danners®. It doesn't matter to the deer. The clicking tines and the grinding horn are the sounds that attract his attention. Nothing else. Here again, this is a classic conditioned response.

Sparring sounds are common in the deer woods every fall and every time a buck investigated the antler noise, he found two bucks making the sounds. When he hears you mimicking the grind and tickle, he fully expects to find the same thing. I have rattled up literally hundreds of deer through the years, mostly with synthetic horns or whatever ingenious rattling devices that were proffered up for me to test. Nearly every one of the bucks responded to a sparring sequence that was performed in a tree stand; twenty feet off the ground. I didn't break limbs or thrash bushes or stomp the ground. The deer don't think "sounds like two bucks but…nah, I don't hear bushes thrashing or limbs breaking and it's too high up." They don't analyze the sound once it is recognized but they can take some precautions.

All out dominant buck fights have some draw backs so I don't like to try to sound like two 900 pound gorillas trying to kill each other. Any buck that thinks he's tough enough to investigate such brutal carrying-on will invariably go down wind before he comes in. In fact, bucks will often scent check any rattling sequence before they commit to an appearance, so keep that in mind when you set up to rattle.

These guys are serious!

Early in the season, my favorite set up is in the edge of an open field with a slight wind in my face. A buck usually won't venture out into the open field in broad daylight to scent check a situation and his curiosity will most likely get the best of him. The closer to the rut you get, the more likely a testosterone driven buck is to forgo caution but you can't count on it. It is always a good idea to set up with a field, a creek, a pond or a bluff directly downwind from your stand. A good calling set up will always discourage scent checking by cautious bucks.

Non-Typical Vocalizations

I'm not going to dispute any manufacturers claims by making disparaging remarks and I'm not selling deer calls or trying to talk you in to or out of anything. I am not opposed to; in fact, I would welcome anything new that would work with any consistency. Since there is no way a human can know exactly how a deer interprets a sound, I have to base my information on educated guesses from past observations. Just seeing something work one time is not enough evidence for me to base a calling strategy on so I'll go over; once again, what I know about deer vocalizations for sure. Deer communicate with one of three voices. They have a larynx or voice box that contains some vocal chords (folds) that generate bleat and bawl sounds. The glottal or grunt sounds are generated by the glottis which is defined as "a combination of the vocal chords and the space in between" and the snorts and sniff sounds that are produced by forcing air through the nasal passages.

When you are calling, it is easy to forget this important detail, so I'll say again; deer use these voices to convey only their most basic emotions. "I'm hurt, I'm scared, I'm lost, I'm mad, come here, and back off". This is about as articulate as they get. These signals can be enhanced with volume and intensity and sequence to convey urgency and there could be some more elaborate subtleties that I'm not aware of but this is what I know What we are talking about in this book are the basics that I am most familiar with. The facts, as I know them, say the known functional deer language is restricted to these confines. Some of this information was discussed in earlier chapters but it is significant enough to bear repeating.

I have heard most of what I call the "wildcat" sounds, in the woods or on videos and they are all, as expected, variations of grunts,   bleats and snorts.

Buck Clicks

The clicking sounds are plainly glottal pulses (grunts) slowed way down for whatever reason. What do they mean? Will they attract other deer? Why? Clicking sounds have been loosely documented on camera on a few occasions, always involving bucks in a courting/chasing mode. My archery wizard buddy Byron Ferguson had such great success making clicking sounds one mid-December morning he thought he was the pied piper. "Bucks were running everywhere and many of them were making the clicks and grunts." He said "Was there any evidence of a hot doe in the area?" I asked "Oh yeah" he said "There was at least one, I saw her run by several times and I thought I heard her bawl a time or two. I figured something must have caught up with her." If any of you have seen the woods "light up" with bucks when a "hot" doe is in the area, especially a full month after the major rut, you know that is a magic time when strange things can happen. I'm not sure if Byron has been able to light that fire again with buck clicks but that one day made a believer out of him. The clicks have the same intonation as the aggravated grunt and their significance escapes me but I will take him at his word and try it myself in the right situation. I have heard deer make those "clicks" but I didn't see other deer responding to them so I haven't concerned myself with trying to imitate them.

Growls and Roars and Bellows

All the information I have on growls and roars and bellows comes from videos produced by call companies promoting product. The live deer sounds I heard on the tapes were distorted or barely audible in most cases and many of the examples were done by humans on "magnum" grunt and bleat calls. The increased volume means the calls will carry farther in the woods but a normal buck that happened to hear a buck Roar, would probably get scared out of two years growth and go so far down wind he would be in a different area code before he got up enough nerve to investigate whatever sounded that big and that bad and that mad. These wildcat vocalizations sound more like abnormalities of aggressive or annoyed grunt and bleat sounds to me and some could be the result of straining or fatigue. They don't serve any distinct biological purpose or convey any unique messages that I know of and they don't say anything that can't be said with the normal voice but what you take to the woods with you is always your choice. I'm still talking "basics" here.

VI. Other Deceptions: Scents, Blinds, and Decoys

Early Deception, Back in the Day

As the fall of 1982 approached, I was eagerly anticipating my second bowhunting season. I had lulled myself into over confidence by putting two nice does in the freezer the previous year while hunting from the ground with a second hand "Whitetail Hunter" compound bow. Now that I was hooked on bowhunting, it was time to take it to the next level.

That year I would be hunting with a new bow, fresh arrows and a brand new, state of the art Baker Self Climbing Tree Stand, complete with a "seat climber" to keep me from having to hug the tree as I climbed. And I wasn't going to mess around with does. I was going after the "big one". The "snaggle-antlered" twelve point non-typical buck that my neighbor called "old Hartford". We had been seeing him off and on for three years, mostly during the late summer and early fall, prowling around the patch of white oak trees that grew on the ridge behind my house. The crafty old rascal would disappear during rifle season when the "blaze oranges" hit the woods but I figured he would be vulnerable during bow season when the acorns started falling. I had already cleared a place on my wall for his antlers, I just had to do a little scouting and plan a strategy. I had permission to hunt the whole ridge but the sixty acres that contained the stand of white oaks was off limits to everyone but me. My neighbor to the north didn't hunt but his son-in-law, Freddie, hunted the 100 acres adjacent to "my" private property just about every weekend during the bow season. Freddie and I weren't friends, in fact we were semi-adversarial since we both hunted the same deer, but we got along. Freddie had been bowhunting for five years when I met him so he was the "senior advisor" in all things bowhunting when we chanced to meet. He stopped by my house-trailer one hot September afternoon with a smug look on his face and a copy of Deer & Deer Hunting magazine in his hand. He said the magazine had just come in the mail and it was the be-all end-all source of information about whitetailed deer. He said he wanted to share some information with me that would help me hunt but I knew he really wanted to show off his expertise. He opened the book to an article on scrapes and rubs and proceeded to tell me all about them and why I should hang my stand close to a well used scrape. I knew about rubs and I was vaguely aware of scrapes but I acted like it was all news to me and graciously accepted his offer to loan me his magazine. I had already been deer hunting for more than twenty years and most of my success had come from hunting over food sources. In spite of this new information, I still planned to hunt "old Hartford" at his dinner table in the white oak stand if the acorns were there. I took binoculars with me when I went scouting the next morning. When I focused them on the treetops I could see the white oaks that had been barren last year were full of acorns and some were already falling. Looking around on the ground I saw the crushed nut shells and droppings that were evidence of heavy deer traffic. I was in the right place. I was looking for a "just right" tree to climb when I noticed a well traveled deer trail that lead from the oaks across the fence onto Freddie's' property. Drat! I hadn't figured Freddie into the mix when I started plotting "old Hartford's" demise but he had to be considered. Freddie did a lot of scouting, he hunted hard and often and he knew about "old Hartford". I would have some competition. Freddie's fence ran East and West along a hollow that was created when the ridge made a U curve to the West. The hollow was two hundred yards deep and about two hundred yards across. From where I stood I could see the deer trail crossing my fence, and then angling toward the back of the hollow. I knew right where the trail was going. To a thicket full of briars and honeysuckle vines that would make a perfect place for "old Hartford" to lay up. I was betting that would be his routine. He would leave the bedding area in the morning, walk the trail for two hundred yards through the hollow, jump the fence, belly out on sweet white oak acorns, and then go back to bed. Just to satisfy my curiosity, I crossed the fence. I was following the trail through the hollow, watching the ground for tracks and droppings, when a shiny piece of metal caught my eye. The piece of metal turned out to be the unpainted head of a carriage bolt that was an integral part of Freddie's climbing tree stand. Daubed in gray and brown paint and covered with brush, Freddie's stand was attached to a red oak tree not far off the deer trail, about twenty yards from my fence. I should have known Freddie would find the trail and the bedding area. Bummer! If I had "old Hartford" figured right, I was cut off.

My spirits were low that evening, thinking about the foiling of all my best laid plans. "Old

Hartford" would have to walk by Freddie to get to me and there wasn't a thing I could do about it. I was thumbing through his copy of Deer & Deer Hunting magazine and cussing my bad luck when I had a flash of inspiration. A plan!

The next morning I hit the woods with some unusual scouting tools. I climbed the fence on to Freddie's property, went across the hollow and around the hill to one of his favorite tree stand sites. I took Freddie's Deer & Deer Hunting magazine out of my back pack, opened it to the scrape article and took a long look at the picture. I found an overhanging limb that looked just right, then I pawed out a buck scrape as big as a car hood right under the limb with the garden rake I had hauled out there for that express purpose. I took the back of my pocket knife and made king sized rubs on several good sized saplings around the scrape, and then made a trail of rubs from the scrape to Freddie's parking place.

Was I being mean and deceitful? Well…maybe a little, but by then I'd become obsessed with "old Hartford" and considered him to be "my buck". I was the one who had figured out the old boy's routine and devised a plan. I had a place for his antlers on the wall and I was the one who created the counterfeit scrape to draw Freddie's attention away from the white oaks. There was nothing illegal about it; I was just doing what had to be done.

I waited until four days before the opening day

of bow season, and then I climbed back over to Freddie's side of the fence. Alright! His stand was gone. After a quiet celebration I took a quick stroll across the hollow to check out my fake scrape. I could see Freddie's stand from a distance, attached to a tree overlooking the mock scrape. I didn't need to get any closer; I beat feet out of there grinning from ear to ear. I went back to the house, grabbed my stand and went back to the white oaks to pick out a tree.

In the crisp pre dawn of opening morning I inched my Baker up a white oak tree and cinched up my safety belt. I pulled up my bow, nocked an arrow, hung the bow on a limb and waited for daylight. I heard a deer crunching acorns below me at first light but I couldn't tell anything about it. As visibility improved, I could see the deer was a decent eight point buck. His antlers had good mass and they were wider than his ears but he wasn't "old Hartford". None of my friends, including Freddie, had ever taken a buck as big as the one that was feeding twenty yards from my tree. I would be a hero if I tagged him and I was sorely tempted but I held out for "old Hartford". As the morning wore on, a steady stream of does and yearlings fed in and out of the oaks. They kept me entertained but no "old Hartford". Finally, after an hour without seeing a deer, I climbed down. As I walked off the ridge I could see Freddie's pick-up coming up my driveway. When I got closer I thought I could see the tips of antlers shining above the truck bed.

It couldn't be, surely not! But it was. "Old Hartford", piled up in the back of Freddie's truck. I felt like I'd been sucker punched right in the gut. Freddie came to meet me as I walked in to the yard. "I got him!" He said "Old Hartford"! "Man, you should have seen him! Just like in the magazine! I was hunting over a scrape as big as a Cadillac car hood. He came in to the scrape right at daylight, put his head down and started pawing, slinging the dirt all over the place. Then he hooked the branches on the limb hanging over the scrape and started biting the twigs. I almost forgot to shoot. "

I congratulated him with my best *anybody could have done it* voice and gave him back his magazine. When he left I took the rake back to the white oak stand and pawed out a scrape as big as a Mack Truck hood but I knew old Hartford wouldn't be back. This was my first attempt to "fool" a deer by using his perception of a situation to manipulate his location. I fooled the wrong one this time but I have since used "mock scrapes" with reliably fresh deer urine to animate and enhance my calling locations.

Ground Blinds: Perception, Deception and Game Changing Innovation

Using artificial calling to attract deer was an eye

opening revelation to me in the mid eighties. Ten years later, innovation and technology delivered another surprising deer hunting appliance that I'm still not totally comfortable with but I can't argue with success. While portable tree stands and deer calls changed the face of deer hunting in the eighties, portable ground blinds came along in the Nineties and added another dimension to fooling the whitetails senses.

Ground blinds may seem to be a little off the subject of calling but we're talking about fooling deer here and taking advantage of gaps in their sense of perception.

I hadn't considered using a ground blind until 1996 when I had an early season lower back episode that ended my tree climbing for that year. I was still eager to be in the deer woods with my bow but I was low on options. I had considered portable ground blinds before and some were available but I was a skeptic. I thought they were awkward and cumbersome and mostly for tourists and small children. I also believed no whitetail in his right mind would ever come close to one. I was commiserating my plight to an archery dealer friend who recommended I watch a video that featured two Minnesota men; Brooks Johnson and Keith Beam, marketing their Double Bull ground blinds. The video demonstrated the blinds' portability, the quick and easy set up and, most impressive to me, amazing footage of Brooks and Keith getting shot after shot on mature whitetail bucks from their ground blinds. They had my attention. After many years of dedicated tree stand hunting, I was about to expand my horizons.

I purchased a Double Bull blind from the dealer and my first set up was a real eye-opener. I set the blind close to a White Oak that was dropping acorns and heavy deer use was evident. After climbing into the dark innards of the blind in full camo, including face mask and gloves, I reared back in a folding chair as comfortable and secure as I would have been in my own office. "Shoot, this can't be hunting," I thought, "it's too easy"! When several does and yearlings came to the oak tree close to my set up to feed, I was even more impressed. They paid no attention to me or to the blind that was sitting less than twenty yards away. While they were close, I got my bow drawn several times, waved my hand and moved around in the blind to see how much activity they would tolerate. They didn't blink an eye. They did spook when I took my glove off and waved my hand through the window outside of the confines of the blind but they returned after a short spell and resumed feeding. I have since used ground blinds many times in situations where tree stands were not a workable option.

Lessons Learned

I've done a lot of calling from blinds with about the same amount of success as calling from tree stands and I've learned a few things along the way. Obviously you want to open the blind windows and make your calls in the direction you think the deer should be coming from. Hanging out the window to do your horn rattling sequences keeps the sound from being muffled and I think the blind walls actually amplify the sound. Some would say calling is more natural coming from ground level which is probably true but I don't think deer analyze altitude when they hear an intriguing sound. Most blinds these days come equipped with shoot through, replaceable window screens. If you use the screens, what you wear in the blind is not that important as long the clothes are dark. If you are shooting a bow through the screens, make sure the screens are tight. A loose screen can alter arrow flight and mechanical broadheads do better when manually expanded before shooting through screens. If you are going to hunt from a blind you should practice shooting from a blind, especially with archery equipment. If you sit sideways to the window you plan to shoot out of, it will help simulate the same position you would be in if you were standing so your shot will be more comfortable. A bow with an arrow nocked on the string is awkward within the confines of the blind unless you are ready to shoot. To avoid poking holes in the blind I lay my bow on the ground beside my chair with an arrow close by. Don't to sit between two open windows (such as front and back) and remember, the enclosure of the blind can create a tunnel effect which can interfere with your ability to judge distance. If cattle are present where you plan to hunt, you should take your blind down at the end of each hunt. Cows seem to be curious about blinds. They can leave it in shambles while satisfying their curiosity.

Comfort is the square root of patience so you should be at least as comfortable as you are in your tree stand so put a comfortable chair in the blind.

Be aware of arrow trajectory, you haven't seen any trajectory like you'll see when an arrow bounces off the frame of a blind window.

If you hunt in the south make sure you don't set your blind over a fire ant bed.

A paperback book will help pass the time but it shouldn't be too compelling. The window of opportunity can be very brief with deer, especially bucks during the rut-be alert! Stay ready!

Exposure to the elements, especially UV rays, will break down the blind fabric and fade the dye if not treated. Protect your investment by treating it with UV blocking chemicals available from ATSKO.

Most of the ground stakes supplied by blind manufacturers are pretty flimsy and easy to lose. Friend and premiere "out west" guide Steve Bishop from Manhattan, Montana, turned me on to using 10" galvanized bridge spikes, available at any hardware store, to stake the blind. If the ground is soft, a boot heel will set the spike, if it is hard you drive them in with a hammer. Steve also says "if you have stakes, use them. A sudden wind gust can pick a blind up and turn it over before you can say tie-down."

Location, Location

I like to set up my blind close to a preferred food source that is showing heavy use. Oaks that are raining acorns, fresh cut corn fields, alfalfa, clover and specifically planted food plots are all great blind locations. You can hunt scrapes and trails if you prefer but the does are coming to the food and the bucks are coming to the does. I used to try to tuck blinds into cover and brush and leaf and limb them until they looked like they were part of the landscape. That was before I talked to an outfitter at one of the hunting shows about blind locations. Mike Wheeler, owner of **Wheeler's Whitetails** told me his clients have taken more than 50 Pope & Young bucks in the last 6 years, including a 200 inch Booner, mostly from ground blinds (in Kansas where climbable trees are scarce). He said he tried brushing in blinds but the deer avoided them so he moved the blinds out into the fields and food plots. He thinks the deer see the blind as another inanimate piece of farm equipment and he believes if a deer can see all the way around a blind, he has no reason to be afraid of it.

He recommends setting blinds at least 10 yards from any heavy cover. I still feel a little exposed but it is hard to argue with success, mine included. I have been more successful hunting from blinds sitting in the bald open than I have in brushed up blinds in cover. I still like to let the blinds sit out for a couple days before I hunt them but that's just me.

What Type of Blind?

A wide variety of portable ground blinds are available on the market today. The competition is intense, so most of them are functional with varying degrees of set-up, transporting and field of view capabilities. Most of the blind walls and ceilings are supported by spring steel or hub-style frames. The spring steel frames are lighter-weight and literally set themselves up if they are folded properly. The hub frames have a hub in each wall and one in the roof. They are heavier and take a little more time to set up but the larger and more stable frame configuration allows for more comfort and a wider viewing area.

More Deception

Tree stands changed the face of bow hunting in the early eighties by moving the hunter above the animal's line of sight. Deer calls enabled the hunter to attract deer by imitating their vocalizations. And lately ground blinds are adding another dimension to effective deer hunting techniques. Ground blinds don't compete with tree stands and they won't replace them in the bowhunters' arsenal but they have several appealing advantages. Once you gain a degree of confidence in blinds, you realize how valuable they can be in grain fields, cut overs, and large food plots where tree stand placement is a problem. They also diminish the impact of adverse weather conditions since they are mostly waterproof and, on bitter cold days, they block the wind and hold in some heat. Beyond the obvious stated advantages, baby-boomer tree-standers like myself, who aren't as athletic as we once were, might choose the comfort and convenience of a ground blind over a tree stand, even when we have a choice. After all, injuries are minimal when you fall out of a ground blind.

Masking, Cover Up and Come Over Here Scents

Whitetails depend on their olfactory senses as much or more than their visual and auditory senses. They might look at something for a time and try to figure out what it is and they may listen to an unusual sound for a while to try to determine if there is reason to flee but one whiff of human scent is all it takes. They depend on their nose without question and their reaction is immediate. One tiny aromatic trace of anything human and they're gone! If we are going to be effective deer hunters, we have to come up with ways to deal with their acute sense of smell. Commercial antidotes are many and varied, the most common being cover scents and scent eliminators. I have first hand stories that illustrate the effectiveness of both cures.

One good example of scent free effectiveness occurred while I was conducting an Outdoor Writers Trophy Bow hunt at Dr. Bob Russell's Heartland Outfitters camp in west central Illinois. One of the writers was at odds with his "dog sitting" live-in girl friend and found it necessary to bring his Labrador Retriever with him to the hunting camp. This writer was an excellent writer, great bow hunter and a real stem winding stickler when it came to scent control. He washed his clothes and his body in odor free soap before each hunt, then stored his clothes in a scent free container and didn't get dressed until he got to the woods. He would stand outside in the bitter cold pulling on his britches and boots, then spray his body and his equipment with whatever "scent killer" was popular at the time. He shot a doe late one evening in the edge of a huge fresh cut corn field but he thought the shot might have been off a little so he thought it better to wait until morning to attempt recovery. The next morning he conspired with his guide to bring his dog "Cody" to the field to find his deer, and then walk Cody thru the woods around the field to possibly push a buck by his stand deep in the woods behind the field.

This account of what occurred that morning came to me person to person from the guide. I have not and won't ever mention it to the writer but he knows his dog's name if he ever reads this book. The guide gave the writer an hour to get situated, then took the dog around the edge of the cornfield. They found the doe 80 yards from where the writer had been hunting the night before, then proceeded as planned. Three hundred yards from the end of the cornfield, Cody threw up his head and took off in a dead run through the woods. The guide followed and found the dog at the foot of the writer's tree, looking up at him and wagging his tail. There was no wind that morning and the writer had approached his stand from a different route so there was no foot scent yet old Cody winded his master three hundred yards away. A Lab's sense of smell pales when compared to that of a deer so I'll let you be the judge as to how effective a "scent-free" regimen is. One more dog story to illustrate scent technology.

It is not as prevalent these days as it once was but there still seems to be a market for *cover* or *masking* scents. Fox and coon urine and skunk scent along with apple, persimmon and acorn fragrances are still assaulting the olfactory senses of the wives of deer hunters who are trying to fool Mother Nature. I was an avid quail hunter back when there were huntable quail populations in Tennessee and me and my crackerjack English setter, Bell Star Crockett, spent many a happy hour pursuing the noble Bob White. One crisp fall morning me and a friend walked up behind a locked up Bell Star and into a large covey of quail that flushed into the wide open blue yonder. In the ensuing episode of gunfire and carnage we managed to bring four of the speeding birds back to earth. Bell lived for and loved to point live quail. She thought it beneath her bearing to snuffle around in the weeds for mangled up dead birds. She would hunt for and find the dead ones after a lot of pleading and scolding but she would always be trying to break free and find an escape route to a fresh bird to point. That morning after a lot of cussing and coaxing she found three of the four downed birds before her selective hearing took over and she took off in the direction the covey had flown. "We might as well go with her" I said, "we'll look for the other one on the way back". We hadn't gone far when Bell came to meet us displaying an embarrassed demeanor that I wasn't used to seeing. As she approached the reason for her self-conscious behavior became obvious. She had blundered into an irritated skunk and taken a full load right in the face. "We have to get her to the truck and get some vinegar and tomato juice on her to kill the odor" I said. She was stinking to high heaven when we walked back through the flush sight but she somehow managed to locate the dead bird we left behind, picked it up and handed it to me. Bell had a great nose, maybe not as precise as a deer but close enough to be comparable.

In spite of have a face and a nose full of pungent, bitter overpowering skunk scent, she was still able to pick up the scent of the dead quail. She smelled the skunk and the quail and whatever other scents were blowing in the wind. I believe a deer smells your cover scent, your armpits and the coffee on your breath all at the same time. The only tried and true solution I know to deal with a deer's scenting ability is to give away any territory directly downwind. The commercially available spray bottles of powder or any other wind direction detection devices can be helpful in letting you know where not to expect a deer to show up but I don't think you can effectively eliminate, mask or cover up human scent to make it undetectable to the nose of a whitetail. There are commercially available scents that are mostly derived from deer urine that can be used to effectively attract deer and the success stories touting various brands are many and varied. As previously stated deer are social animals and being so, they are interested in others of their kind. There are all kinds of claims from manufacturers about where the urine came from and how it was gathered and what state of estrous the doe was in when it was bottled (at the exact moment she was ready to stand still for the buck??). These claims are impossible to verify and the more bizarre the claims, the more they charge you for a tiny bottle full.. I have seen deer urine on the shelves at Wal_Mart and having dealt with them when I was in the call business; I know how huge the initial order is from Wal-Mart. If anyone has a deer herd large enough to produce that much urine (forty or fifty thousand bottles for the initial order) you would think some of us would have heard about it. Where does it come from? That being said, I will say a bow hunting friend had placed a scent container full of one of the Wal-Mart brands of "Doe-in Heat" scent close to his stand in the Alabama deer woods one January morning. When a mature buck made the mistake of coming within bow range of my friends' stand, he made a good shot that mortally wounded him. The buck bolted at the shot but came to a halt at the scent container, curled his upper lip in a classic Fleming posture and fell over dead. What can you say? I've had some success with attractive urine scents and I have had deer walk by my scent station without notice. I don't think urine in any form will alarm a deer, just try to make sure it is this year's batch. Old urine smells more like ammonia. The woods are full of scents from animal waste and deteriorating plant matter of varying ages and volumes so most animals probably ignore a scent that is non-threatening. If it works for you, use it. When it comes to the expensive kind remember, there is no truth in advertising law when it comes to deer scent. They can put anything on the bottle even if it came from the men' and you can't deny or verify their claims. Think about it!

Visual Deception

Decoys are another very distinctive form of visual deception. The realistic models can be very effective but decoys haven't had the success and acceptance that deer calls and scents have enjoyed. Enough people use them with enough success to create a kind of a niche market but there are several commonly perceived problems with decoys. They are expensive, awkward to move and set up and their appearance isn't precise enough for the human eye. Be that as it may, a decoy can be a real game changer if you are hunting big crop fields. Most of the decoys come with removable antlers so the hunter can choose between a passive or an active scenario. I prefer using the doe to trigger the mating anticipation response since it is such a powerful response any little glitches in my set up, imagined or real could be overlooked in the heat of passion.

VII. Tips to Increase Your Calling Success

Be Ready!

"He was huge!" the excited deer hunter exclaimed, holding his hands about two feet apart, "he came straight to the call and stopped broadside, not 20 yards from my stand". "Great" I said, "did you bring a picture with you?" "You're not going to believe this" he said with a sheepish grin "I hadn't seen anything all morning so I let my bow down and started to unfasten my safety belt. I remembered my brand new, never used deer call and thought what the heck. I let go with a couple obscene parting shots on the call before I climbed down and the buck of a lifetime came boiling out of the brush like his tail was on fire. He stopped broadside, twenty yards from my stand and I'm holding 25 feet of rope with my bow tied on the other end!" I had this conversation at one of the early "Deer Classics" and I have had many more like it since. I believed him.

This hunter's experience was not that unusual, especially for first time callers or callers trying a new technique. With no confidence in the call or the technique, he's thinking "I never heard a deer make a sound like that" or "this will probably run off anything within hearing". He has no idea what he is saying when he makes the call. He has no clue what it should sound like and/or he has never had a deer respond to calling so he has no real reason to believe his deer call will work. Some of his buddies say they have called deer doing this and that but he isn't too sure about them either so he sets himself up for failure by making a call and not expecting anything to show up. I can't begin to tell you how many tales of woe I've heard from seasoned deer hunters who missed out on golden opportunities because their brains were on pause when a buck showed up. If you believe in something enough to buy it and haul it to the woods with you, then you should believe something is going to happen when you use it. Remember, you aren't trying to call him up in the tree with you. You just want the deer to come into the area to investigate the deer making the calls. He may come in hard and fast or he may slip in and be gone before you know he was there. Make the call; then wait for him! Look for Him! Stay on "red alert" for 15 or 20 minutes after you make the call. Expect a response and anticipate success! You will still get caught with your guard down from time to time but you won't feel so dumb about it.

Consistently successful callers (deer, elk, turkey, etc.) always anticipate success and prepare for a response. This anticipation is what I call the confidence factor and it usually comes from experience and a working knowledge of the language. You don't have to learn the hard way. Learn the language and when you make a deer call expect a deer to show up. Be ready!

When You See a Deer

Deer have big ears. They are good at pinpointing the precise location of a sounds' origin so my rule is: If you can see a deer coming toward you, let him come, even if he is dawdling and taking his time. You are in good shape as long as he is headed your way. If you make a sound while he is en route you will call his attention to your location and increase the possibility of getting picked off and that means game over. If the deer veers off in another direction, a soft doe or buck grunt could be the right invitation to put him back on course. If he is not heading my way, I'll call to any deer I see wandering around but I keep it soft and passive unless I see or hear a buck trailing a doe. When that happens, I'm going to get more aggressive with some heavy breathing doe bleats to try to turn his head. I have called several bucks to me that were trailing does because they thought the bleating doe was the same one they were trailing. You don't have anything to lose in those situations.

When you are doing blind calling, always take a hard look around before you make a call to be sure the immediate area is clear of deer that could bust you and ruin your hunt. If you get busted, let him go. There's no reason to call to a deer that you know you have spooked. He won't come back once he has you pegged and he might very well associate the call to humans. What do you think he will do the next time he hears a call?

Learn the Language

Before you start blowing on your deer call you should make sure you know what you are saying so you don't say the wrong thing at the wrong time. As previously discussed, new calls and calling techniques come and go and some of them may merit some attention. Deer can't change their language so just be sure you are familiar with the basics. Beyond that, you have to be the judge of what is right for you. Knowing the right sound to make to trigger a specific response gets you in the game. Making the proper sound in the correct sequence gives you a chance to score.

Set Up to Call

Do your calling in a high deer use area where deer are comfortable making and responding to calls. You are not going to call many deer in the Wal-Mart parking lot or when they are alarmed or distressed. An important, but often overlooked aspect of calling success is in the caller's location and set-up. "What do you do when a buck comes almost close enough to shoot and won't come any closer?" I wish I had a quarter for every time I've been asked that question. The reason he won't come any closer is because he can't see the deer he's been hearing. He wants visual reinforcement to the audio signals he's been getting. He could have sworn he heard a deer but he can see where the sound came from and he can't see a deer. He's looking hard so if you call to him while he's looking in your direction (he usually will be if he's responding to a call), he'll most likely look you right in the eye and the hunt will be over. Your best bet is to let him walk, then try to call him back when he gets out of sight. If you plan to call, try to position your stand on a rise or in some thick stuff so the deer will be in range when he comes into view. Don't forget, if you're going to do some aggressive calling or horn rattling; always try to set up with a natural barrier downwind from your stand. If you can keep a buck from scent checking your position when responding to the calling, your chances for success are much better, especially with older deer.

Be Familiar with Your Calls and Have a Plan (Basics Review)

Deer calls are not high performance instruments. They don't require a lot of precise tonal breath control and you won't have to practice much on a decent call to get it sounding right. You should, however, make sure it is in working order before you get to the woods with it. You should also have some notion of how to control the volume and the tone of the call. Volume is especially important since it can totally change the meaning of a call. As earlier discussed, a low volume monotone grunt is a social sound that is reassuring to other deer while a loud drawn out grunt is an aggressive, aggravated sound that can intimidate or alarm deer.

I always have a plan that involves a calling

strategy, no matter where or when I am hunting. It can vary with the situation and the rut stage and it may not work on a given day, but a plan gives me a starting point. On early fall hunts I like to set up close to food sources and make an occasional soft buck grunt. This call can arouse curiosity and reassure any deer within hearing that this area is secure. This is where accuracy is important. If your call sounds enough like a deer and you can positively establish the fact that there is a least one relaxed deer in the area, you have a big foot in the door. An occasional call means one soft grunt every 10 or fifteen minutes.

As the days get shorter and the leaves start turning, I'll bring grunt calls, rattling horns, and doe bleat calls to the stand with me. I'll start off with some trailing grunts to wake up the woods and try to get a buck fired up. I'll do a series of fifteen or twenty grunts, randomly spaced, while turning my head slowly as I call to suggest movement. If nothing shows up in fifteen or twenty minutes I'll try some doe bleats. Four to six urgent contact bleats at random intervals. I'll repeat the sequence every ten or fifteen minutes for an hour or so. If nothing responds, I'll try some light sparring and soft buck grunts. I'll continue calling off and on as long as conditions are favorable. The best time to call deer is when they can hear you. Most days that means early morning or late evening but if the winds stay calm, I'll continue calling until I have to get down out of the tree. I've had great success calling deer up in the middle of the day when the weather permitted.

Around the middle of November, in most parts of the country, the rut is in full swing. Bucks are chasing does and breeding does and looking for does. If you can catch a buck when he is lusting after does, an urgent doe bleat should bring him on the run. When you hear a buck grunting while he is trailing a doe that is you cue to play him some doe music. He's looking for a doe and he isn't sure where she went. If you say the right thing at the right time you sure won't run anything off. When the plan works and all the pieces come together, you will have the makings of a great story.

Don't Over-Anticipate

Expect a response but don't be crushed if it doesn't happen. A lot of things have to be in place for a deer to respond to calling. If the rut is on, a buck is not likely to respond to any kind of calling unless he is between does. Some bucks are more aggressive than others and more likely to respond to aggressive calling or rattling during the pre-rut while the sub dominant and less aggressive bucks are more drawn to less intimidating social sounds. There are also times when none of them seem to want to respond to anything. Remember, survival is the deer's number one priority, if they are threatened or suspicious or stressed in any way, social behavior takes a back seat to their survival instincts.

Don't Get Discouraged

Using a deer call is kind of like using a favorite fishing lure. It worked well in the past, and then one day you beat the water white with it and not a nibble. Do you throw it away? Of course not. You pack it up and come back and try it another day.

Think about what you are doing when you use your deer call. You now know why deer respond to calling and what sounds to make to trigger those responses. If your calling is based on sound biological strategies and you are accurately producing the right sounds, you should see some results. Don't be concerned if nothing shows up. If you can't call him, another deer couldn't call him! Come back and try him again on another day.

Deer calls can be effective tools to augment and enhance the deer hunting strategies and techniques that you already have in place. They are not substitutes for proper stand placement or scent control and they won't consistently overcome sloppy hunting habits. There are no magic bullets that I know of. You don't have to use deer calls to be a successful deer hunter but calling adds an element of increased excitement and a new dimension of personal involvement to deer hunting. You are communicating with another species in their language and trying to manipulate them to your advantage.

Once you get it right and make it happen, calling will become an integral part of your deer hunting tactics and techniques. The thrill of a buck responding to your calling is an experience you won't forget as long as you live and you're going to want to try to make it happen again every time you go deer hunting. If you're going to use deer calls, do it on purpose. *Learn the language, develop a strategy, set up properly and anticipate success.*

Be safe and good luck hunting and calling!

Made in the USA
Charleston, SC
31 December 2015